Sacred Alchemy

A collection of Qur'anic Verses

Commentary by Shaykh Fadhlalla Haeri
Translation reviewed by Dr Adnan al Adnani
Compiled and Produced by Leyya Kalla

By Quintessence Publishing
E-mail: info@qpublish.com
www.qpublish.com

Revised Edition Published in 2017

© Quintessence Publishing

All rights reserved. Except for brief quotations in critical articles or reviews,
no part of this book may be reproduced in any manner without prior written
permission from Quintessence Publishing.

Typeset in South Africa by Quintessence Publishing
Cover Calligraphy image by Mohamed Ehsai
Cover Design by Leyya Kalla & Mizpah Marketing Concepts

ISBN 978-0-620-71182-1

Acknowledgements

I would like to acknowledge the past and present masters of the alchemy of inner transformation.

Sincere thanks to Shaykh Ahmed Haeri Mazanderani and his son Shaykh Fadhlalla Haeri who continue their good works in the way of Allah, in the seen and unseen worlds.

Sacred Alchemy

Dedication

This booklet is dedicated to the greatest inspirations in my life, may peace and blessings be upon this heavenly family; the beloved Prophet Mohammed, Fatimah Zahra, Imam Ali ibn Abi Talib, Imam Hussan ibn Ali and Imam Hussein ibn Ali.

Sincere thanks to my family and friends for their unconditional love and support. May the Light of Al-Qur'an illumine our way in this life and the next, inshallah.

Sacred Alchemy

Introduction

For those seeking a deeper understanding as to the meaning of life, our purpose on earth, the nature of happiness and the quest for inner peace, life can be end up being a confusing and challenging story to unravel.

It is easy to get lost and out of balance if we dont possess a clear reference. Keeping the company of like-minded friends, constant reflection and remembrance of the Higher Truth in ritual and practice and the benefit of a true spiritual guide are amongst the necessary elements toward gaining deeper insights.

The Qur'an is the ultimate reference guide in revealing these hidden and manifest truths, but to approach this sacred text with the correct courtesy and be granted its secrets requires an open and sincere heart, a clear mind and a courage to face Reality and the truth of one's present state. The Qur'an acts as a mirror in which one can guage their present level of awareness.

Sacred Alchemy

This booklet first began as a rough collection from the teachings and advice received from my teacher, Shaykh Fadhlalla Haeri and was later extended in conjuction with him to include additional verses and commentary. His light has taught me that divine light is everpresent and that in truth, the Light of the Qur'an reveals nothing but perfection in God's great theatre.

These Qur'anic reminders have helped me to nourish my heart and mind with the everprevalent Truth of the One and Only One — Allah.

May you benefit from reading them as well, inshallah.

Leyya Kalla

December 2017

Qur'anic Verses

Approach these verses with a sincere heart, an open mind and a clean body.

Then take permission from The One on High and ask permission to allow the alchemical effects of this most Sacred Book to transform you.

We begin in the name of Allah, the Most Merciful. Bismillah hirrahman nirrahim.

Sacred Alchemy

16:18

If you were to count Allah's blessings, you could not take stock of them. Allah is All-Forgiving, Compassionate to each.

Commentary

Divine Grace permeates the universe and is experienced as events. Therefore, these blessings are endless and cannot be counted.

Qur'anic Verses

55:1-4

The All-Merciful! Taught the Quran. He created man. He taught him eloquence..

COMMENTARY

Events within space and time appear in steps, with a beginning and an end. The Book of Reality, the Qurán, contains all that there is, known and unknown, in the universe.

This Book of Reality is revealed and taught in conjunction with the creation of human beings following by discriminination and discernment.

Sacred Alchemy

55:53

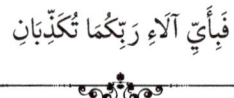

Which, then, of your Lord's blessings do you both deny?

COMMENTARY

All signs and manifestations are from Allah and thus none of them can be denied.

Qur'anic Verses

39:53

$$\text{قُلْ يَا عِبَادِيَ الَّذِينَ أَسْرَفُوا عَلَى أَنْفُسِهِمْ لَا تَقْنَطُوا مِنْ رَحْمَةِ اللَّهِ ۚ إِنَّ اللَّهَ يَغْفِرُ الذُّنُوبَ جَمِيعًا ۚ إِنَّهُ هُوَ الْغَفُورُ الرَّحِيمُ}$$

Say: "O My servants who have transgressed against themselves, do not despair of Allah's mercy. Allah forgives all sins: He is All-Forgiving, Compassionate to each.

COMMENTARY

To experience right and wrong is a natural human condition. The right emanates from the soul but body, mind and emotions can be a barrier resulting in errors.

Sacred Alchemy

93:3

Your Lord has not forsaken you, nor disdains.

COMMENTARY

The original Sacred Light is everpresent. There is no separation between the subject and the master.

Qur'anic Verses

49:13

يَا أَيُّهَا النَّاسُ إِنَّا خَلَقْنَاكُم مِّن ذَكَرٍ وَأُنثَىٰ وَجَعَلْنَاكُمْ شُعُوبًا وَقَبَائِلَ لِتَعَارَفُوا ۚ إِنَّ أَكْرَمَكُمْ عِندَ اللَّهِ أَتْقَاكُمْ ۚ إِنَّ اللَّهَ عَلِيمٌ خَبِيرٌ

O mankind, We created you male and female, and made you into nations and tribes that you may come to know one another. The noblest among you in Allah's sight are the most pious. Allah is All-Knowing, All-Experienced.

COMMENTARY

Human manifestation is due to the Sacred Light which brings about increase and variation in creation. The purpose of which is to have the discipline of cautious awareness and responsibility to the Origin.

Sacred Alchemy

18:7

We have appointed all that is on the earth for an adornment for it, and that We may try which of them is fairest in works.

COMMENTARY

Existence on earth has numerous attractions and there is always that which is repulsive. The human mind is designed to choose that which is the best.

Qur'anic Verses

30:42

قُلْ سِيرُوا۟ فِى ٱلْأَرْضِ فَٱنظُرُوا۟ كَيْفَ كَانَ عَـٰقِبَةُ ٱلَّذِينَ مِن قَبْلُ ۚ كَانَ أَكْثَرُهُم مُّشْرِكِينَ

Say: "Journey in the land and observe the fate of those who came before — most have not been in Unity" (Tawhid).

COMMENTARY

We naturally try to learn from the past to avoid serious damage and mistakes. The ultimate destructiveness is due to the lack of direction and experience of cosmic Oneness.

Sacred Alchemy

30:41

ظَهَرَ الْفَسَادُ فِي الْبَرِّ وَالْبَحْرِ بِمَا كَسَبَتْ أَيْدِي النَّاسِ لِيُذِيقَهُمْ بَعْضَ الَّذِي عَمِلُوا لَعَلَّهُمْ يَرْجِعُونَ

Corruption has appeared on land and sea because of what people's hands have earned. He will make them taste part of what they have committed; perhaps they will turn back.

COMMENTARY

All errors and mistakes will appear to us in different ways. We will be afflicted by them so that we remain in awareness not to repeat our distractions and errors.

Qur'anic Verses

30:7

They know an outward part of the present life, but of the Hereafter they are heedless.

COMMENTARY

Whatever appears to us makes its impact upon our senses and mind. All emanates from the unseen which will be fully experienced in the Hereafter.

Sacred Alchemy

11:24

The likeness of the two groups is like the blind and deaf, and the one who sees and hears: are they equal in likeness? Will you not reflect?

COMMENTARY

Our wakeful life has numerous degrees of enlightenment. At one end are those who are like sleepwalkers and at the other end, those who are fully awake to reality.

Qur'anic Verses

39:9

اَمَّنْ هُوَ قَانِتٌ اٰنَآءَ الَّيْلِ سَاجِدًا وَقَآئِمًا يَحْذَرُ الْاٰخِرَةَ وَيَرْجُوا رَحْمَةَ رَبِّهٖ قُلْ هَلْ يَسْتَوِى الَّذِيْنَ يَعْلَمُوْنَ وَالَّذِيْنَ لَا يَعْلَمُوْنَ اِنَّمَا يَتَذَكَّرُ أُولُوا الْاَلْبَابِ

Or is he who is devout in the watches of the night, bowing himself and standing, he being vigilant of the world to come and hoping for the mercy of his Lord . . ? Say: 'Are they equal -- those who know and those who know not?' Only men possessed of the kernal of insight remember.

COMMENTARY

Effort to go beyond the limitation of mind and reason is needed to awaken. Spiritual seekers need regular exercise of night vigil and transcendence, whilst maintaining purity at heart.

Sacred Alchemy

39:29

ضَرَبَ ٱللَّهُ مَثَلاً رَّجُلاً فِيهِ شُرَكَآءُ مُتَشَٰكِسُونَ وَرَجُلاً سَلَمًا لِّرَجُلٍ هَلْ يَسْتَوِيَانِ مَثَلاً ٱلْحَمْدُ لِلَّهِ بَلْ أَكْثَرُهُمْ لَا يَعْلَمُونَ

Allah sets forth an example: There is a man in whom are (several) partners differing with one another, and there is another man wholly owned by one man. Are the two alike in condition? (All) praise is due to Allah. Nay! most of them do not know.

COMMENTARY

To have one clear direction, path and master, will lead to success. Otherwise confusion and chaos will be destructive.

Qur'anic Verses

23:53

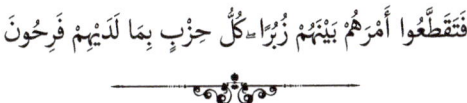

But they split in their affair between them into sects, each party rejoicing in what is with them.

COMMENTARY

It is natural for us to be pleased with what we do and who we are, good or bad.

Sacred Alchemy

70:19-21

إِنَّ الْإِنْسَانَ خُلِقَ هَلُوعًا

إِذَا مَسَّهُ الشَّرُّ جَزُوعًا

وَإِذَا مَسَّهُ الْخَيْرُ مَنُوعًا

Man was truly created anxious, whenever misfortune touches him, he is filled with self-pity; and whenever good fortune comes to him, he withholds it.

COMMENTARY

It is in the nature of human beings to be impatient—the soul is ever constant and beyond time. Thus whenever we are at ease we desire to preserve and continue it, and become exasperated with afflictions.

Qur'anic Verses

30:11

Allah originates creation, then restores it, and then to Him you shall be returned.

COMMENTARY

It all begins from the source and returns back to it.

Sacred Alchemy

29:64

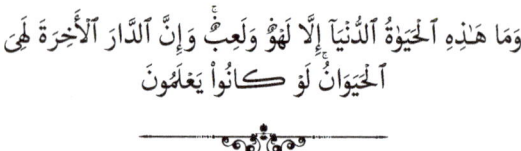

This present life is nothing but frivolity and amusement. But the Abode of the Hereafter is the real life, if only they knew!

COMMENTARY

Life on earth is like a playground for us to move higher in consciousness. In the Hereafter, there are no distractions or confusions that can mask the brilliant soul.

Qur'anic Verses

87:6

We shall make you read so as not to forget.

COMMENTARY

The human soul knows the truth and if we read through the lens of our soul, all becomes clear and evident.

8:35

$$\text{وَمَا كَانَ صَلَاتُهُمْ عِندَ الْبَيْتِ إِلَّا مُكَاءً وَتَصْدِيَةً ۚ فَذُوقُوا الْعَذَابَ بِمَا كُنتُمْ تَكْفُرُونَ}$$

Their prayers before the House are nothing but noise and clapping. 'So taste the chastisement for your denial.'

COMMENTARY

Religious rituals are to lead towards awakening to the truth rather than just frivolous exercises.

Qur'anic Verses

15:19

وَالْأَرْضَ مَدَدْنَٰهَا وَأَلْقَيْنَا فِيهَا رَوَاسِيَ وَأَنۢبَتْنَا فِيهَا مِن كُلِّ شَىْءٍ مَّوْزُونٍ

As for the earth, We have spread it out, set firm anchors in it, and made everything grow there in due balance.

COMMENTARY

The evolution of the earth over millennia brought about the balance that enabled life to be established where there are no longer any sensory advantages.

Sacred Alchemy

17:72

Whoso is blind in this world, in the Hereafter he shall be even more blind and more astray from the path.

COMMENTARY

Whoever is blind (to meanings and insights) in this world will be more blind in the next world.

Qur'anic Verses

22:46

أَفَلَمْ يَسِيرُوا فِي الْأَرْضِ فَتَكُونَ لَهُمْ قُلُوبٌ يَعْقِلُونَ بِهَا أَوْ آذَانٌ يَسْمَعُونَ بِهَا ۖ فَإِنَّهَا لَا تَعْمَى الْأَبْصَارُ وَلَٰكِنْ تَعْمَى الْقُلُوبُ الَّتِي فِي الصُّدُورِ

What, have they not journeyed in the land so that they have hearts to understand with or ears to hear with? It is not the eyes that are blind, but blind are the hearts that turn away.

COMMENTARY

Travel and exploration on earth enables the heart to evolve and hearing to reveal inner meanings. Sight is important in the sensory realm, but it is insight due to the soul within the heart that matters most.

2:213

كَانَ النَّاسُ أُمَّةً وَاحِدَةً فَبَعَثَ اللَّهُ النَّبِيِّينَ مُبَشِّرِينَ وَمُنذِرِينَ وَأَنزَلَ مَعَهُمُ الْكِتَابَ بِالْحَقِّ لِيَحْكُمَ بَيْنَ النَّاسِ فِيمَا اخْتَلَفُوا فِيهِ...

Mankind was a single community, then Allah sent prophets to bring good news and warning, and with them He sent the Book with the Truth, to judge between people in their disagreements.

COMMENTARY

The origin of mankind is One. As humanity spread, from amongst them comes guidance to what is just so that disagreements may lead to understanding and acceptance.

Qur'anic Verses

30:36

وَإِذَآ أَذَقْنَا النَّاسَ رَحْمَةً فَرِحُوا بِهَا وَإِنْ تُصِبْهُمْ سَيِّئَةٌ بِمَا قَدَّمَتْ أَيْدِيهِمْ إِذَا هُمْ يَقْنَطُونَ

And when We let men taste mercy, they rejoice in it; but if some evil befalls them for that their own hands have brought forth, behold, they despair.

COMMENTARY

The self always looks for expansion and increase and celebrates comfort and ease. It tries to avoid restrictions and difficulties.

Sacred Alchemy

16:61

وَلَوْ يُؤَاخِذُ اللَّهُ النَّاسَ بِظُلْمِهِمْ مَا تَرَكَ عَلَيْهَا مِنْ دَابَّةٍ وَلَٰكِنْ يُؤَخِّرُهُمْ إِلَىٰ أَجَلٍ مُسَمًّى ۖ فَإِذَا جَاءَ أَجَلُهُمْ لَا يَسْتَأْخِرُونَ سَاعَةً ۖ وَلَا يَسْتَقْدِمُونَ

If Allah were to hold mankind to account for their wrongdoing, He would not leave alive one single creature that treads the earth. He merely defers them until a stated time. When their time arrives they can neither delay it nor bring it forward, even by an instant.

COMMENTARY

Action and reaction are always in perfect balance. The reaction to much of our human action is postponed, otherwise life will cease to exist. We are always given time to reflect and repent.

Qur'anic Verses

21:35

Every self shall taste death. We put you to the test, with evil and good, as an ordeal. And to Us you shall return.

COMMENTARY

Death is a natural experience that we will all go through. All human experiences considered good or bad challenge us towards transcendence of our sensory values.

Sacred Alchemy

42:23

ذَٰلِكَ الَّذِي يُبَشِّرُ اللَّهُ عِبَادَهُ الَّذِينَ آمَنُوا وَعَمِلُوا الصَّالِحَاتِ ۗ قُل لَّا أَسْأَلُكُمْ عَلَيْهِ أَجْرًا إِلَّا الْمَوَدَّةَ فِي الْقُرْبَىٰ ۗ وَمَن يَقْتَرِفْ حَسَنَةً نَّزِدْ لَهُ فِيهَا حُسْنًا ۚ إِنَّ اللَّهَ غَفُورٌ شَكُورٌ

These are the glad tidings that Allah conveys to His worshippers, to them who are faithful and righteous in deeds. Say 'I ask you no wage for it save amity of kinship. Whoso performs a goodly deed, to him We shall increase it in goodness. Allah is All-Forgiving, All-Thankful'.

COMMENTARY

A prophetic being who is in constant reference to the Divine Source is not looking for reward from others. What he hopes for is simply courtesy and kindness towards those who are close to the prophetic way.

Qur'anic Verses

76:3

إِنَّا هَدَيْنَاهُ السَّبِيلَ إِمَّا شَاكِرًا وَإِمَّا كَفُورًا

We guided him upon the way, be he grateful or ungrateful.

COMMENTARY

Guidance is already there through the soul, but a few are in gratitude and others are in denial and loss.

Sacred Alchemy

2:216

You may dislike something although it is good for you, or like something although it is bad for you: Allah knows and you do not.

COMMENTARY

The self is a shadow of the soul and by its nature it is confused and wayward and may like a thing which is not conducive for its surrender to the soul. It also dislikes what often can lead it to unity with the soul.

Qur'anic Verses

9:40

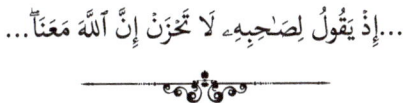

It was then that he said to his companion: 'Do not grieve, for Allah is with us.'

COMMENTARY

Prophetic light reveals, at all time, the divine presence within the heart.

29:3

$$\text{وَلَقَدْ فَتَنَّا الَّذِينَ مِنْ قَبْلِهِمْ ۖ فَلَيَعْلَمَنَّ اللَّهُ الَّذِينَ صَدَقُوا وَلَيَعْلَمَنَّ الْكَاذِبِينَ}$$

We put to the test those who came before them, that Allah may know who were sincere and who were lying.

COMMENTARY

Earthly tests and afflictions are part of the nature of earthly reality. It is through these afflictions that we will come to know the truth.

Qur'anic Verses

80:24

Let man consider his food.

COMMENTARY

To reflect upon one's provisions, whether air, food or other, will reveal the self's dependence and its desire to be free from needs as the soul is.

Sacred Alchemy

55:46

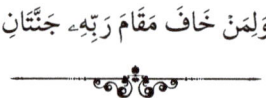

And for him who fears to stand before his Lord are two gardens.

COMMENTARY

All earthly experiences are metaphors for the Hereafter. Our love for gardens on earth is a prelude to experiencing the eternal garden in the Hereafter.

Qur'anic Verses

6:152

Be fair in weights and measures, and act equitably. We charge no self except what it can bear.

COMMENTARY

Reason and rationality is exercised by thinking and acting appropriately. Every thing or situation has a balance and appropriate position.

Sacred Alchemy

2:189

...وَلَٰكِنَّ الْبِرَّ مَنِ اتَّقَىٰ ۗ وَأْتُوا الْبُيُوتَ مِنْ أَبْوَابِهَا ۚ وَاتَّقُوا اللَّهَ لَعَلَّكُمْ تُفْلِحُونَ

So enter your houses by their doors and be mindful of Allah so that you may prosper.

COMMENTARY

Every situation has its key and the appropriate courtesy to enter a house is to go through the door, not through a window or illicit means.

Qur'anic Verses

23:102

Then he whose scales are heavy - they are the prosperers.

COMMENTARY

Good actions and appropriate living is considered as weighty and important. This metaphor implies an appropriate ending and success to such living.

Sacred Alchemy

6:160

مَن جَآءَ بِٱلْحَسَنَةِ فَلَهُ عَشْرُ أَمْثَالِهَا ۖ وَمَن جَآءَ بِٱلسَّيِّئَةِ فَلَا يُجْزَىٰٓ إِلَّا مِثْلَهَا وَهُمْ لَا يُظْلَمُونَ

Whoso brings a good deed shall have ten the like of it; and whoso brings an evil deed shall only be recompensed the like of it; they shall not be wronged.

COMMENTARY

Bad action begets its equivalent of bad results whereas good action brings about tenfold of goodness.

Qur'anic Verses

8:70

…إِنْ يَعْلَمِ اللَّهُ فِي قُلُوبِكُمْ خَيْرًا يُؤْتِكُمْ خَيْرًا مِمَّا أُخِذَ مِنْكُمْ وَيَغْفِرْ لَكُمْ ۗ وَاللَّهُ غَفُورٌ رَحِيمٌ

'If Allah knows of any good in your hearts, He will give you more than what was captured from you, and will forgive you — He is All-Forgiving, Compassionate to each.

COMMENTARY

The nature of a pure heart is such that even in a situation of a loss it will be replaced with a better gain.

Sacred Alchemy

14:34

$$\text{وَآتَاكُم مِّن كُلِّ مَا سَأَلْتُمُوهُ ۚ وَإِن تَعُدُّوا نِعْمَتَ اللَّهِ لَا تُحْصُوهَا ۗ إِنَّ الْإِنسَانَ لَظَلُومٌ كَفَّارٌ}$$

Who granted you all you asked of Him. Were you to count the bounties of Allah, you could not take stock of them. Mankind is indeed wicked and most ungrateful.

COMMENTARY

Goodness and grace upon us is immeasurable as we are granted our desires.

Qur'anic Verses

6:126

This is the path of thy Lord; straight; We have distinguished the signs to a people who remember.

COMMENTARY

Spiritual signs and insights can benefit those who are reflective—remembering the divine origin of all.

3:117

..and Allah is not unjust to them, but they are unjust to themselves.

COMMENTARY

The path of reality is smooth and perfect. It is the confusion of the self that causes distortions and suffering.

Qur'anic Verses

42:30

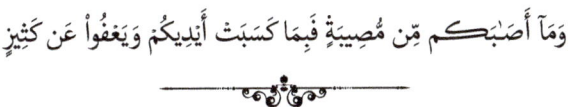

Whatever affliction may visit you is for what your own hands have earned; and He pardons much.

COMMENTARY

It is through ignorance and lack of clarity that we bring upon ourselves affliction.

Sacred Alchemy

3:191

الَّذِينَ يَذْكُرُونَ اللَّهَ قِيَامًا وَقُعُودًا وَعَلَىٰ جُنُوبِهِمْ وَيَتَفَكَّرُونَ فِي خَلْقِ السَّمَاوَاتِ وَالْأَرْضِ رَبَّنَا مَا خَلَقْتَ هَٰذَا بَاطِلًا سُبْحَانَكَ فَقِنَا عَذَابَ النَّارِ

Those who remember Allah standing, sitting, and lying down, who reflect on the creation of the heavens and earth: 'Our Lord! You have not created all this without purpose– You are far above that! So protect us from the torment of the Fire'.

COMMENTARY

Through a spiritual path, a sincere seeker will be in a state of constant remembrance of God and through this reference, earthly experiences will flow smoothly.

Qur'anic Verses

65:2-3

...ذَٰلِكُمْ يُوعَظُ بِهِ مَنْ كَانَ يُؤْمِنُ بِاللَّهِ وَالْيَوْمِ الْآخِرِ ۚ وَمَنْ يَتَّقِ اللَّهَ يَجْعَلْ لَهُ مَخْرَجًا

وَيَرْزُقْهُ مِنْ حَيْثُ لَا يَحْتَسِبُ ۚ وَمَنْ يَتَوَكَّلْ عَلَى اللَّهِ فَهُوَ حَسْبُهُ ۚ إِنَّ اللَّهَ بَالِغُ أَمْرِهِ ۚ قَدْ جَعَلَ اللَّهُ لِكُلِّ شَيْءٍ قَدْرًا

Anyone who believes in Allah and the Last Day should heed this:

Allah will find a way out for those who are cautiously aware of Him, and shall provide for him from where he never imagined. Whoso places his trust in Allah, Allah shall suffice him. Allah enforces what He commands. For all things. Allah has set a measure.

COMMENTARY

Whoever is in cautious awareness and remembrance of Allah will be shown the way and provided for from the unseen. Allah will attain His purpose (to be known).

Sacred Alchemy

4:58

Indeed Allah orders you to render the trusts to their owners.

COMMENTARY

The most precious thing in life is life itself which we have been entrusted with for a while and returning it to its rightful owner is our supreme duty.

Qur'anic Verses

32:21

وَلَنُذِيقَنَّهُم مِّنَ ٱلْعَذَابِ ٱلْأَدْنَىٰ دُونَ ٱلْعَذَابِ ٱلْأَكْبَرِ لَعَلَّهُمْ يَرْجِعُونَ

We shall make them taste the lesser torment rather than the greater — perchance they might return.

COMMENTARY

On this earth we experience samples of fires and the garden, whereas in the Hereafter it is the immense fire and the perfect garden.

Sacred Alchemy

83:14

كَلَّا بَلْ رَانَ عَلَى قُلُوبِهِم مَّا كَانُوا يَكْسِبُونَ

No indeed! Their hearts are encrusted with what they have earned.

COMMENTARY

When the heart is veiled its light does not shine or lead and therefore the path is confused.

Qur'anic Verses

94:7-8

فَإِذَا فَرَغْتَ فَانْصَبْ

وَإِلَىٰ رَبِّكَ فَارْغَبْ

When your work is done (emptied/freed), rise in devotion, and turn to your Lord for everything.

COMMENTARY

When your body is healthy and your mind is clear, then one is poised for a spiritual uplift.

Sacred Alchemy

3:101

Whoever holds fast to Allah will be guided to the straight path.

COMMENTARY

Creation is based upon signs and designs of the creator and it is only those without insight who are in ignorance and denial.

Qur'anic Verses

2:183

يَٰٓأَيُّهَا ٱلَّذِينَ ءَامَنُواْ كُتِبَ عَلَيْكُمُ ٱلصِّيَامُ كَمَا كُتِبَ عَلَى ٱلَّذِينَ مِن قَبْلِكُمْ لَعَلَّكُمْ تَتَّقُونَ

O You who have attained faith! Fasting is ordained for you as it was ordained for those before you, so that you might remain conscious of Allah.

COMMENTARY

Absention and restriction of human tendencies are necessary for the process of openings of the Higher.

Sacred Alchemy

16:90

إِنَّ ٱللَّهَ يَأْمُرُ بِٱلْعَدْلِ وَٱلْإِحْسَٰنِ وَإِيتَآئِ ذِى ٱلْقُرْبَىٰ وَيَنْهَىٰ عَنِ ٱلْفَحْشَآءِ وَٱلْمُنكَرِ وَٱلْبَغْىِ يَعِظُكُمْ لَعَلَّكُمْ تَذَكَّرُونَ

Allah commands justice, virtue and generosity to kin. He forbids debauchery, abomination and injustice. He counsels you; perhaps you may remember.

COMMENTARY

Creation floats upon goodness, mercy and grace. When we acknowledge and embrace these qualities, we flow according to the nature of creation and will thus be more likely to awaken to the origin and meaning of it all.

Qur'anic Verses

2:170 -171

وَإِذَا قِيلَ لَهُمُ اتَّبِعُوا مَا أَنزَلَ اللَّهُ قَالُوا بَلْ نَتَّبِعُ مَا أَلْفَيْنَا عَلَيْهِ آبَاءَنَا ۚ أَوَلَوْ كَانَ آبَاؤُهُمْ لَا يَعْقِلُونَ شَيْئًا وَلَا يَهْتَدُونَ

وَمَثَلُ الَّذِينَ كَفَرُوا كَمَثَلِ الَّذِي يَنْعِقُ بِمَا لَا يَسْمَعُ إِلَّا دُعَاءً وَنِدَاءً ۚ صُمٌّ بُكْمٌ عُمْيٌ فَهُمْ لَا يَعْقِلُونَ

And when it is said to them, Follow what Allah has revealed, they say: Nay! we follow what we found our fathers upon. What! and though their fathers had no sense at all, nor did they follow the right way.

The parable of those who reject faith is as if one were to shout like a goat-herd, to things that listen to nothing but calls and cries; deaf, dumb, and blind. They are void of wisdom.

Commentary

It is natural for human beings to repeat and follow traditions, some of which are good and others not necessarily so. Habits that lead to higher consciousness are condoned.

Sacred Alchemy

84:6

يَٰٓأَيُّهَا ٱلْإِنسَٰنُ إِنَّكَ كَادِحٌ إِلَىٰ رَبِّكَ كَدْحًا فَمُلَٰقِيهِ

Oh humans, indeed you are labouring toward your Lord with exertion and will meet Him.

COMMENTARY

The human self can lead to the soul and can also be an obstacle.

Qur'anic Verses

36:22

And why should I not serve Him who originated me, and unto whom you shall be returned?

COMMENTARY

The spiritually intelligent being wants to worship that which is worthy and from which everything emanates and returns.

Sacred Alchemy

64:11

مَآ أَصَابَ مِن مُّصِيبَةٍ إِلَّا بِإِذْنِ ٱللَّهِ وَمَن يُؤْمِنْ بِٱللَّهِ يَهْدِ قَلْبَهُ ۚ وَٱللَّهُ بِكُلِّ شَىْءٍ عَلِيمٌ

Misfortunes can only happen with Allah's permission - He will guide the heart of anyone who believes in Him: Allah knows all things.

COMMENTARY

It is through trust and reliance upon God that afflictions will be put in perspective and guidance will be given or received.

Qur'anic Verses

92:5-7

فَأَمَّا مَنْ أَعْطَىٰ وَاتَّقَىٰ

وَصَدَّقَ بِالْحُسْنَىٰ

فَسَنُيَسِّرُهُ لِلْيُسْرَىٰ

As for him who gives and is dutiful (toward Allah), and believes in the best, Surely We will ease his way unto the state of ease.

COMMENTARY

To be generous and in constant awareness of God, will pave the way towards an easy life.

Sacred Alchemy

51:20-21

وَفِي الْأَرْضِ آيَاتٌ لِلْمُوقِنِينَ

وَفِي أَنْفُسِكُمْ ۚ أَفَلَا تُبْصِرُونَ

And on earth there are signs for those who are certain in faith, and in yourselves, do you not then see?

COMMENTARY

Signs of connectedness and direction in creation are everywhere, especially within human beings aspiring for the ultimate at all times.

Qur'anic Verses

55:29

يَسْأَلُهُ مَنْ فِي السَّمَاوَاتِ وَالْأَرْضِ ۚ كُلَّ يَوْمٍ هُوَ فِي شَأْنٍ

Whoever is in the heavens and the earth implore Him. Every day He is upon some task.

COMMENTARY

Human needs are endless and the desire to be satisfied and content by Grace is constant.

Sacred Alchemy

93:11

And as for the favours of your Lord, speak of it.

COMMENTARY

The more we remember grace and generosity, the more likely we will also allow it to flow from us.

Qur'anic Verses

7:180

وَلِلَّهِ الْأَسْمَاءُ الْحُسْنَىٰ فَادْعُوهُ بِهَا وَذَرُوا الَّذِينَ يُلْحِدُونَ فِي أَسْمَائِهِ ۚ سَيُجْزَوْنَ مَا كَانُوا يَعْمَلُونَ

And Allah's are the fairest names, therefore call on Him thereby, and leave alone those who violate the sanctity of His names; they shall be recompensed for what they do.

COMMENTARY

All desirable attributes and divine qualities are like ladders that we can adhere to and climb to the Source.

Sacred Alchemy

7:56

وَلَا تُفْسِدُوا۟ فِى ٱلْأَرْضِ بَعْدَ إِصْلَٰحِهَا وَٱدْعُوهُ خَوْفًا وَطَمَعًا إِنَّ رَحْمَتَ ٱللَّهِ قَرِيبٌ مِّنَ ٱلْمُحْسِنِينَ

Do not corrupt the land once it has been set right. Call upon Him in piety and in hope, for the mercy of Allah is within reach of the righteous.

COMMENTARY

After a few billion years, life began on earth. We contain the possibility of the Highest in consciousness. Care, sensitivity and respect are necessary for evolvement and growth towards awakening.

Qur'anic Verses

2:3

Those who have faith in the unseen and keep up prayer and spend out of what We have given them.

COMMENTARY

Our human physical and biological nature will lead us to the desire to explore the unseen, which is vast and infinite. Belief and trust in the unknown, whilst acting as best as possible, within the norm, is the foundation of the path.

Sacred Alchemy

18: 67-68

قَالَ إِنَّكَ لَنْ تَسْتَطِيعَ مَعِيَ صَبْرًا

وَكَيْفَ تَصْبِرُ عَلَىٰ مَا لَمْ تُحِطْ بِهِ خُبْرًا

He said: Surely you cannot have patience with me, And how can you have patience for what you do not encompass in knowledge?

COMMENTARY

Enlightened Prophet Khidr knew that Musa was eager to exercise his wisdom and therefore will be impatient with his actions. One can only be patient in a situation that one understands.

Qur'anic Verses

40:60

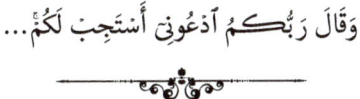

And your Lord says: Call upon Me, I will answer you..

COMMENTARY

Our needs propels us to hope and expect fulfilment. That is the path to higher consciousness.

Sacred Alchemy

7:96

وَلَوْ أَنَّ أَهْلَ الْقُرَىٰ آمَنُوا وَاتَّقَوْا لَفَتَحْنَا عَلَيْهِمْ بَرَكَاتٍ مِنَ السَّمَاءِ وَالْأَرْضِ وَلَٰكِنْ كَذَّبُوا فَأَخَذْنَاهُمْ بِمَا كَانُوا يَكْسِبُونَ

Had the people of the cities become faithful and grown conscious of us, We would have opened to them the blessings of heaven and earth. But they rejected truth, so We seized them in recompense for what they earned.

COMMENTARY

Human nature contains the divine light and if we live by that, perfection prevails.

Qur'anic Verses

7:156

...وَرَحْمَتِي وَسِعَتْ كُلَّ شَيْءٍ ۚ فَسَأَكْتُبُهَا لِلَّذِينَ يَتَّقُونَ وَيُؤْتُونَ الزَّكَوٰةَ وَالَّذِينَ هُم بِـَٔايَـٰتِنَا يُؤْمِنُونَ

...My mercy encompasses all things. 'I shall ordain My mercy for those who are conscious of Allah and pay the prescribed alms; who believe in Our Revelations'.

COMMENTARY

Everything in existence is permeated by God's mercy and grace which can only be witnessed and experienced by those who are in the highest state of consciousness and God awareness.

Sacred Alchemy

57:28

يَٰٓأَيُّهَا ٱلَّذِينَ ءَامَنُوا۟ ٱتَّقُوا۟ ٱللَّهَ وَءَامِنُوا۟ بِرَسُولِهِۦ يُؤْتِكُمْ كِفْلَيْنِ مِن رَّحْمَتِهِۦ وَيَجْعَل لَّكُمْ نُورًا تَمْشُونَ بِهِۦ وَيَغْفِرْ لَكُمْ وَٱللَّهُ غَفُورٌ رَّحِيمٌ

Oh Faithful, be mindful of Allah and have faith in His messenger. He will give you a double share of his mercy; he will provide a light to help you walk; he will forgive you – Allah is most Forgiving, most Merciful.

COMMENTARY

The fruit of faith, trust and following the prophetic path is to be guided by divine light and experiencing double goodness, as everything in existence is based on duality.

Qur'anic Verses

11:108

وَأَمَّا الَّذِينَ سُعِدُوا فَفِي الْجَنَّةِ خَالِدِينَ فِيهَا مَا دَامَتِ السَّمَٰوَٰتُ وَالْأَرْضُ إِلَّا مَا شَاءَ رَبُّكَ ۖ عَطَاءً غَيْرَ مَجْذُوذٍ

And those who are blessed shall be in the Garden: They will dwell therein for all the time that the heavens and the earth endure, except as thy Lord will, a gift without break.

COMMENTARY

The state of the perfect garden and bliss is an energy field that is both on earth and in heavens. To qualify entry, one has to lose identity and be at one with Sacred Reality.

24:21

يَا أَيُّهَا الَّذِينَ آمَنُوا لَا تَتَّبِعُوا خُطُوَاتِ الشَّيْطَانِ ۚ وَمَن يَتَّبِعْ خُطُوَاتِ الشَّيْطَانِ فَإِنَّهُ يَأْمُرُ بِالْفَحْشَاءِ وَالْمُنكَرِ ۚ وَلَوْلَا فَضْلُ اللَّهِ عَلَيْكُمْ وَرَحْمَتُهُ مَا زَكَىٰ مِنكُم مِّنْ أَحَدٍ أَبَدًا وَلَٰكِنَّ اللَّهَ يُزَكِّي مَن يَشَاءُ ۗ وَاللَّهُ سَمِيعٌ عَلِيمٌ

O faithful, follow not the steps of Satan; for whosoever follows the steps of Satan, assuredly he bids to indecency and dishonour. But for Allah's Grace to you and His mercy not one of you would have been pure ever; but Allah purifies whom He wills; and Allah is All-Hearing, All-Knowing.

COMMENTARY

The light of God's grace and mercy has its shadow which can mislead and bring about a state of hell. Constant vigilance is necessary.

Qur'anic Verses

6:54

كَتَبَ رَبُّكُمْ عَلَىٰ نَفْسِهِ ٱلرَّحْمَةَ ۖ أَنَّهُ مَنْ عَمِلَ مِنكُمْ سُوٓءًا بِجَهَٰلَةٍ ثُمَّ تَابَ مِنۢ بَعْدِهِۦ وَأَصْلَحَ فَأَنَّهُۥ غَفُورٌ رَّحِيمٌ

And when those who have faith in Our signs come to thee, say, 'Peace be upon you.' Your Lord has prescribed for Himself mercy. Whosoever of you does evil in ignorance, and thereafter repents and makes amends, He is All-forgiving, compassionate to each.

COMMENTARY

Humans are prone to errors and deviations. Divine Grace is everpresent whenever repentance and vigilance is exercised.

Sacred Alchemy

7:99

Do they really feel secure from the planning of Allah? None can feel secure from the planning of Allah save those who are lost.

COMMENTARY

Allah's ways are beyond human comprehension and it is a serious fault if anyone ever thinks that they are not subject to the infinite unseen. Much of human life is an unintended consequence of thoughts and actions which have no reference to the Higher.

Qur'anic Verses

4:135

يَاأَيُّهَا الَّذِينَ آمَنُوا كُونُوا قَوَّامِينَ بِالْقِسْطِ شُهَدَاءَ لِلَّهِ وَلَوْ عَلَىٰ أَنْفُسِكُمْ...

You who have faith, uphold justice and bear witness to Allah, even if it is against yourselves...

COMMENTARY

Justice implies full witnessing and understanding a situation. Its foundation is self-awareness and transparency.

Sacred Alchemy

2:18

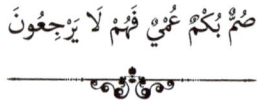

Deaf, dumb, blind, they will not return (to the path).

COMMENTARY

The lowest stage of human beings are those who are deaf, dumb and blind of insight and are unable to return to Divine consciousness.

Qur'anic Verses

2:9

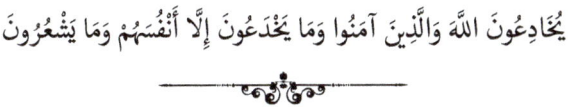

They desire to deceive Allah and those who believe, and they deceive only themselves and they do not perceive.

COMMENTARY

Deceiving others implies self-deception. This is not easy to be aware of. One needs to step out of oneself to witness the self.

Sacred Alchemy

79:37- 41

فَأَمَّا مَنْ طَغَىٰ

وَآثَرَ الْحَيَاةَ الدُّنْيَا

فَإِنَّ الْجَحِيمَ هِيَ الْمَأْوَىٰ

وَأَمَّا مَنْ خَافَ مَقَامَ رَبِّهِ وَنَهَى النَّفْسَ عَنِ الْهَوَىٰ

فَإِنَّ الْجَنَّةَ هِيَ الْمَأْوَىٰ

Whoso then has exceeded all bounds; And prefers the life of this world; Surely Hell shall be the abode. But as for him who feared the Station of his Lord and forbade the soul its caprice, surely Paradise shall be the abode.

COMMENTARY

Our short life on earth is a prelude and preparation for the hereafter. Otherwise it is full of suffering and destruction.

Qur'anic Verses

89:27-28

يَا أَيَّتُهَا النَّفْسُ الْمُطْمَئِنَّةُ

ارْجِعِي إِلَى رَبِّكِ رَاضِيَةً مَرْضِيَّةً

Oh contented self! Return to your Lord, well-pleased, well-pleasing.

COMMENTARY

When the self is tethered and has yielded to the soul, it will experience a direct connection to the sacred origin. It will thus experience the rewards of worship and the garden.

Sacred Alchemy

7:205

وَاذْكُر رَّبَّكَ فِي نَفْسِكَ تَضَرُّعًا وَخِيفَةً وَدُونَ الْجَهْرِ مِنَ الْقَوْلِ بِالْغُدُوِّ وَالْآصَالِ وَلَا تَكُن مِّنَ الْغَافِلِينَ

And remember your Lord within yourself humbly and fearing and in a voice not loud in the morning and the evening and be not of the heedless ones.

COMMENTARY

Distraction from constant awareness of divine presence can be overcome by the discipline of constant awareness of higher consciousness in all situations.

Qur'anic Verses

70:32

And those who are faithful to their trusts and their covenant.

COMMENTARY

The path towards knowledge of the One begins with being authentic and acting as one with regard to promises and trustworthiness.

Sacred Alchemy

20:12

Surely I am your Lord, therefore take off your shoes; you are in the sacred valley, Tuwa.

COMMENTARY

When the voice of Truth is heard, the response of the soul is such that the self loses identity and the need to be protected or saved.

Qur'anic Verses

27:40

Whosoever gives thanks, gives thanks only for his own self's good, and whosoever is ungrateful - my Lord is surely All-Sufficient, All-Noble.

COMMENTARY

The human quest for goodness is ultimately for the self to be at one with the ultimate divine gift of the soul within. Gratitude and contentment can only increase that goodness. The reverse is also against self-evolvement.

Sacred Alchemy

50:33

Who held the Most Gracious in awe, unseen, who comes before Him with a heart turned to Him in devotion.

COMMENTARY

Spiritual evolvement is accompanied by constant cautious awareness, and a heart that refers to God.

Qur'anic Verses

14:7

وَإِذْ تَأَذَّنَ رَبُّكُمْ لَئِنْ شَكَرْتُمْ لَأَزِيدَنَّكُمْ ۖ وَلَئِنْ كَفَرْتُمْ إِنَّ عَذَابِي لَشَدِيدٌ

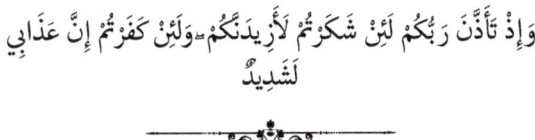

And when your Lord proclaimed, "If you are thankful, surely I will increase you, but if you are thankless My chastisement is surely severe."

COMMENTARY

Gratitude and awareness of divine grace will only bring increase in spiritual states otherwise afflictions will only increase.

Sacred Alchemy

51:56

وَمَا خَلَقْتُ الْجِنَّ وَالْإِنْسَ إِلَّا لِيَعْبُدُونِ

I created jinn (the hidden) and mankind only to worship Me.

COMMENTARY

The prescribed path is to be in a high state of transformative worship.

Qur'anic Verses

10:62

Surely the friends of Allah — no fear shall fall upon them, nor shall they grieve.

COMMENTARY

Fear and sorrow are two major human obstacles. It is those who yearn for God who will be spared.

Sacred Alchemy

53:9

Until he was two bow-lengths away or even closer.

COMMENTARY

The illumined being will experience being enclosed by the Real.

Qur'anic Verses

41:53

We shall show them Our wonders on all horizons and in their selves, until it becomes obvious to them that it is the Truth. Does it not suffice that your Lord is a witness of all things?

COMMENTARY

Signs of divine presence are in every situation, at all times and at all levels, including high horizons.

Sacred Alchemy

3:154

$$...وَلِيَبْتَلِيَ اللّٰهُ مَا فِي صُدُورِكُمْ وَلِيُمَحِّصَ مَا فِي قُلُوبِكُمْ وَاللّٰهُ عَلِيمٌ بِذَاتِ الصُّدُورِ$$

And that Allah might test what was in your hearts and that He might purge what was in your hearts; and Allah knows what is in the hearts.

COMMENTARY

A big puzzle and challenge in life is to realise that nothing can happen unless it is willed and allowed by God, at the same time each human being does have a connection with one's own destiny but it is so subtle that it is not easily realised. Much of it is subconscious. Much of it is just glimpses of things that we desire secretly but eventually what we experience is that which is divinely accepted and ordered. It may be against one's wish and hope. It may be with one's own expectation.

Qur'anic Verses

4:111

وَمَن يَكْسِبْ إِثْمًا فَإِنَّمَا يَكْسِبُهُۥ عَلَىٰ نَفْسِهِۦ وَكَانَ ٱللَّهُ عَلِيمًا حَكِيمًا

He who commits a misdeed does so against his own self – Allah is All Knowing and Wise.

COMMENTARY

The human project on earth is to realise the essence and existence of life which is the soul itself. Whatever we earn of good or bad it is for or against one's own self. You are the project in that you are consciously or otherwise developing.

Sacred Alchemy

2:115

The East and the West belong to Allah: wherever you turn, there is His Face. Allah is All-Pervading and All-Knowing.

COMMENTARY

Creation is entirely from the One, by the One unto the One. Wherever you turn you are facing an aspect of the One and only One and as such whatever there is known and unknown belongs and is under the control of the One.

Qur'anic Verses

20:46

He said: "Fear not, for I am with you, I hear and see (everything)."

COMMENTARY

When all the shadows and illusions are discarded then you know that you are here seeing, hearing and moving by Allah. Therefore, you know that Allah is with you, before you, within you and after you. As such human fears, anxiety and sorrows will disappear.

Sacred Alchemy

51:22

And in heaven is your sustenance, as (also) that which you are promised.

COMMENTARY

Whatever we experience on our little earth and the terrestrial realm has its root in the celestial. Whatever there is on earth is from the heavens. Whatever is physical, chemical and material is from the pure energy source which engulfs all. Our provisions and needs are also emanating from the unseen and experienced by us who straddle the seen and the unseen.

Qur'anic Verses

56:62

وَلَقَدْ عَلِمْتُمُ النَّشْأَةَ الْأُولَىٰ فَلَوْلَا تَذَكَّرُونَ...

You know all about the first creation — will you not remember and reflect?

COMMENTARY

Within our soul lies the original spark of existence, as such within us lies a deep memory of the beginning of it all.

Sacred Alchemy

29:2

Do the people think that they will be left to say, "We believe" and they will not be tried?

COMMENTARY

The challenge of life is to be integrated as one being. You are one in truth but most of the time we experience multiplicities because your mind oscillates between telling you something and then changing it to something else, thus the danger of hypocrisy and as such, life's experience will expose us so that you end up being one as far as your intention, attention and innermost is concerned. The experience of life will polish us to be authentic and in a unitive state.

Qur'anic Verses

55:60

Shall the reward of good be anything but good?

COMMENTARY

When you move up the ladder of consciousness and you begin to see and experience perfection and goodness irrespective of the judgement of the mind of good or bad, then only goodness will emanate from you. If you are a recipient of unconditional love and generosity, then you too will reflect that goodness and justice.

Sacred Alchemy

16:97

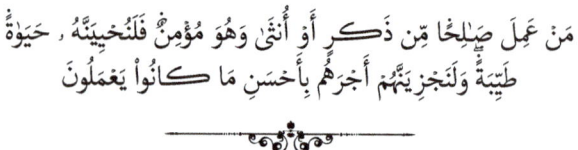

Whoever does good, male or female, while having faith, We shall make him live a decent life, and We shall recompense them with their wages, in accordance with the best of their deeds.

COMMENTARY

Thinking good, acting good, intending good and all of the refinement we hope to bring about in our conduct, and all the virtuous deeds and activities we aspire for, will take us to the borderline of pure consciousness. We are all struggling in conditioned consciousness, limited consciousness, human consciousness and it is not good enough. What we hope and desire to is access to a consciousness that is ever-perfect, ever-constant and that is often related to as another state of life and that is a quantum change from the relative world we are living in.

Qur'anic Verses

45:15

مَنْ عَمِلَ صَالِحًا فَلِنَفْسِهِ ۖ وَمَنْ أَسَاءَ فَعَلَيْهَا ۖ ثُمَّ إِلَىٰ رَبِّكُمْ تُرْجَعُونَ

Whoso does righteousness, it is to his own gain, and whoso does evil, it is to its own loss; then to your Lord you shall be returned.

COMMENTARY

Any good action in the sense of its quality of generosity and goodness will bring goodness upon the person who perpetrates it and vice versa. Goodness is the origin of creation and the ultimate all-encompassing field of energy emanating from the Creator.

Sacred Alchemy

55:7

He has raised up the heavens. He has set the balance.

COMMENTARY

Everything within the world of existence is in balance. Every action has an equal and opposite reaction and the higher you go in consciousness the subtler that balance will be until such time that it reaches the point of or the middle point between the two sides of the balance. That doesn't move. It is constant and steady.

Qur'anic Verses

73:5

Behold, We shall cast upon thee a weighty word.

COMMENTARY

As we grow in consciousness and we mature we can take, understand and accept difficult positions and major challenges. Ultimately the heaviest impartation of the unseen or God's revelation is that you as an independent entity do not exist, this is considered a most weighty impartation or word.

Sacred Alchemy

14:1

بِسْمِ اللَّهِ الرَّحْمَٰنِ الرَّحِيمِ الر ۚ كِتَابٌ أَنزَلْنَاهُ إِلَيْكَ لِتُخْرِجَ النَّاسَ مِنَ الظُّلُمَاتِ إِلَى النُّورِ بِإِذْنِ رَبِّهِمْ إِلَىٰ صِرَاطِ الْعَزِيزِ الْحَمِيدِ

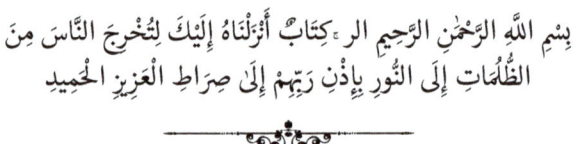

Alif. Lam. Ra. A Book has been revealed to you [Mohammed], so that, by the permission of their Lord, you would be able to lead people from darkness into light along the path of the Majestic, Praised-One.

COMMENTARY

The entire human journey from beginning to end on this earth is like moving in a tunnel of mist and darkness. If you are on a path, if you are watchful or avoiding that which is dark, negative, egotistical or from your physical animal past than you are moving towards light until such time you see by that Sacred Light. Initially that light appears occasionally as a spark somewhere in the dim distance but the entire journey is from utter darkness to less until you find there is only divine and sacred light.

Qur'anic Verses

2:138

Receive the colouring attributes of Allah, and who is better than Allah in attributing? And Him do we serve.

COMMENTARY

Allah's qualities and attributes are like ladders that we aspire to acquire. Generosity, goodness, beauty, power, strength, knowledge and on and on. So if you take some of these colours upon you as a human being than your humanity will enable you to rise with these ladders on these steps towards a divinity which lies within you anyway.

Sacred Alchemy

2:54

وَإِذْ قَالَ مُوسَىٰ لِقَوْمِهِ يَا قَوْمِ إِنَّكُمْ ظَلَمْتُمْ أَنْفُسَكُم بِاتِّخَاذِكُمُ الْعِجْلَ فَتُوبُوا إِلَىٰ بَارِئِكُمْ فَاقْتُلُوا أَنْفُسَكُمْ ذَٰلِكُمْ خَيْرٌ لَكُمْ عِندَ بَارِئِكُمْ فَتَابَ عَلَيْكُمْ ۚ إِنَّهُ هُوَ التَّوَّابُ الرَّحِيمُ

And when Moses said unto his people: "O my people! Verily, you have wronged against yourselves by worshipping the calf; turn, then in repentance to your maker and mortify yourselves; this will be the best for you in your Maker's sight. And thereupon He accepted your Rrepentance: for, behold, He alone is the Acceptor of Repentance, the Dispenser of Grace.

COMMENTARY

Ultimately the injustice we perpetrate upon ourselves is to imagine the independence that we have from cosmic reality or God. This is the ultimate crime upon ourselves and others. Not unless the self has been put at rest, we remain always with a tarnish of illusions, delusions and injustices.

Qur'anic Verses

2:185

Allah wants ease for you, not hardship.

COMMENTARY

The path of awakening is the path of ease and every difficulty is to do with the lower self and trying to groom it or fall under its darkness.

Sacred Alchemy

33:72

إِنَّا عَرَضْنَا الْأَمَانَةَ عَلَى السَّمٰوٰتِ وَالْأَرْضِ وَالْجِبَالِ فَأَبَيْنَ أَنْ يَحْمِلْنَهَا وَأَشْفَقْنَ مِنْهَا وَ حَمَلَهَا الْإِنْسَانُ إِنَّهُ كَانَ ظَلُومًا جَهُولًا ۙ

We offered the trust to the heavens, the earth and the mountains, but they declined to carry it and were afraid of it, but man carried it — and he has ever been unjust, intemperate.

Commentary

The nature of the soul or spirit is so immense that it contains the same dimensions and meaning of that of the entire cosmos. Therefore, this mysterious reality which we call self or soul or spirit cannot resonate with any material or earthly matter but the human state and the human psyche is such that it can be that we have this potential or this soul, yet we remain worse than animals. The soul is like the ultimate treasure and a gift that we are given as a custodian. It belongs to the one and only all-encompassing Reality or Truth – Allah.

Qur'anic Verses

49:7

$$\text{وَاعْلَمُوْا اَنَّ فِيكُمْ رَسُوْلَ اللّٰهِ لَوْ يُطِيْعُكُمْ فِيْ كَثِيْرٍ مِنَ الْاَمْرِ لَعَنِتُّمْ وَلٰكِنَّ اللّٰهَ حَبَّبَ اِلَيْكُمُ الْاِيْمَانَ وَزَيَّنَهُ فِيْ قُلُوْبِكُمْ وَكَرَّهَ اِلَيْكُمُ الْكُفْرَ وَالْفُسُوْقَ وَالْعِصْيَانَ اُولٰٓئِكَ هُمُ الرّٰشِدُوْنَ}$$

And know that among you is Allah's Messenger; should he obey you in many a matter, you would surely fall into distress, but Allah has endeared the faith to you and has made it seemly in your hearts, and He has made hateful to you unbelief and transgression and disobedience; these it is that are the followers of a right way.

COMMENTARY

Trust, love, adherence to a path and continuing a familiar line, is a most desirable state to be in. Therefore, deep down in every heart we love to have faith, trust and to do our work on this short journey. Getting out of our own darkness towards light is the cause of our experiencing darkness.

Sacred Alchemy

55:19

He has made the two seas to flow freely (so that) they meet together.

COMMENTARY

Everything in existence is based on two complementary realities. Within us is a meeting point of the two infinite oceans. One of them is that which is constant and is absolute and is not subject to any definitions, Supreme consciousness, Pure consciousness and the other side is ever-changing consciousness, human consciousness, conditioned consciousness.

Qur'anic Verses

3:169

وَلَا تَحْسَبَنَّ الَّذِينَ قُتِلُوا فِي سَبِيلِ اللَّهِ أَمْوَاتًا ۚ بَلْ أَحْيَاءٌ عِنْدَ رَبِّهِمْ يُرْزَقُونَ

Do not think of those slain for the cause of Allah as dead. They are alive with their Lord and receive sustenance from Him.

COMMENTARY

And leaving life or dying whilst you are pursuing the awakening process to truth does not in any way undermine arrival of that truth. Life is not yours, you are a custodian of it. If it is lost in a cause of justice then there is no loss in it.

Sacred Alchemy

17:44

$$\text{تُسَبِّحُ لَهُ السَّمَاوَاتُ السَّبْعُ وَالْأَرْضُ وَمَن فِيهِنَّ ۚ وَإِن مِّن شَيْءٍ إِلَّا يُسَبِّحُ بِحَمْدِهِ وَلَٰكِن لَّا تَفْقَهُونَ تَسْبِيحَهُمْ ۗ إِنَّهُ كَانَ حَلِيمًا غَفُورًا}$$

The seven heavens and the earth sing His praises, and all who are therein. There is nothing that does not sing His praise, but you do not understand their songs of praise. Surely He is All-Forbearing, All-Forgiving.

COMMENTARY

Whatever that exists — seen, known or unknown — resonates with its origin and destiny and that is termed as glorification. It is in fact responding to its reality. Every leaf, every tree, every insect resonates with its situation to maintain life that is within it. Everyone is obsessed with life as it appears to them.

Qur'anic Verses

53:10

And he revealed to His servant what He revealed.

COMMENTARY

All our sensory connections respond to the environment, and are aspects of the universal connectivity that we have. Intuition and other extra-sensory impacts upon us are part of higher consciousness. Ultimately pure inspiration that comes through the heart is one of these numerous different states or stages of signals that come from the infinite unknown.

Sacred Alchemy

53:11

The heart was not untrue in (making him [Mohammed] see) what he saw.

COMMENTARY

The innermost of your heart knows the truth whereas the heart can sometimes be sick, it can sometimes be under duress. It is the innermost light that does not have any shadow and is connected to its origin which is the Sacred Light of Allah. The state of after-life is available here in this life. It's the state where there is no fear or anxiety or association with body, biography or identity if you travel on this earth without a desire to be in control, create mischief and follow other egotistic tendencies.

Qur'anic Verses

28:83

تِلْكَ الدَّارُ الْآخِرَةُ نَجْعَلُهَا لِلَّذِينَ لَا يُرِيدُونَ عُلُوًّا فِي الْأَرْضِ وَلَا فَسَادًا ۚ وَالْعَاقِبَةُ لِلْمُتَّقِينَ

As for that life in the hereafter, We grant it to those who do not seek to exalt themselves on earth, nor yet to spread corruption: for the future belongs to the Allah-conscious.

COMMENTARY

The next phase of life, which is boundless in space and in time, is inseperable from the short-lived earthly life. When the lower side of human consciousness is tethered and the ego is groomed, then access to the Hereafter becomes a natural confirmation of our destination. All belongs to Allah.

Sacred Alchemy

42:20

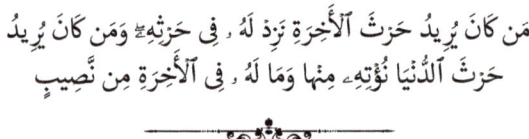

Whoso desires the tillage of the Hereafter, We double his tillage; Whoso desires the tillage of this world, We provide him of it, but he has no share in the Hereafter.

COMMENTARY

Human life on this earth gives each one of us the apparent choice that we either get more of this world, more accumulation, more wealth, more power, more status or we want to be liberated from all the concerns of dualities which often cause nothing other than confusion and conflict. If you want the earthly accumulation and power you will be given it and you may get nothing after your death and vice versa.

Qur'anic Verses

50:21

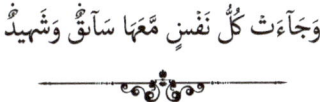

And every soul shall come, and with it a driver and a witness.

COMMENTARY

There are numerous forces and powers that drive us. These are the driving forces in life. Every instant in your life has a witness that tells you what your real intention and direction is. If you give attention to the witnessing power within you, that will be a radar for you that guides you towards the purpose of your own life which is to Life itself.

Sacred Alchemy

30:19

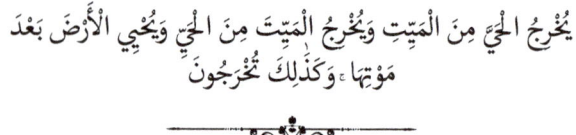

He brings forth the living from the dead and the dead from the living; He revives the earth after its death, and thus will you too be brought forth.

COMMENTARY

The cyles of birth and death are like many other patterns in life, which are repetitive. The earth was an accumulation of cosmic debris, but life took root on it as part of the cycle of the disintegration of everything on earth. The same applies to an emergence of consciousness after the end of physical creation.

Qur'anic Verses

27:4

إِنَّ ٱلَّذِينَ لَا يُؤْمِنُونَ بِٱلْأَخِرَةِ زَيَّنَّا لَهُمْ أَعْمَٰلَهُمْ فَهُمْ يَعْمَهُونَ

As for those who are not faithful in the Hereafter, We have made their deeds seem alluring to them, so they wander blindly.

COMMENTARY

Faith and belief may lead to awakening to the truth of the Hereafter. If we do not awaken, we may succumb to infatuation with earthly illusions and delusions.

Sacred Alchemy

11:15

مَنْ كَانَ يُرِيدُ الْحَيَاةَ الدُّنْيَا وَزِينَتَهَا نُوَفِّ إِلَيْهِمْ أَعْمَالَهُمْ فِيهَا وَهُمْ فِيهَا لَا يُبْخَسُونَ

Whoso desires this nether world and its luxuries, to them We pay in full their works therein, and in it they shall not be short-changed.

COMMENTARY

Those beings who are limited in intelligence and consciousness, and are only concerned with earthly life, will experience what they had desired.

Qur'anic Verses

40:39

يَا قَوْمِ إِنَّمَا هَٰذِهِ الْحَيَاةُ الدُّنْيَا مَتَاعٌ وَإِنَّ الْآخِرَةَ هِيَ دَارُ الْقَرَارِ

O my people! This life of the world is only a (passing) enjoyment, and surely the Hereafter is the abode to settle.

COMMENTARY

Our life on earth is a prelude and a sample of the Hereafter. This short, earthly experience naturally leads to a zone that is perpetual and permanent.

Sacred Alchemy

11:105

On the day when it shall come, no soul shall speak except with His permission, then (some) of them shall be wretched and (others) happy.

COMMENTARY

If you have not practiced connection with higher consciousness in this life you will be completely at a loss after death. The more you practice in this earth the more you will be flowing with ease and comfort after death.

Qur'anic Verses

36:65

اَلْيَوْمَ نَخْتِمُ عَلَىٰ اَفْوَاهِهِمْ وَتُكَلِّمُنَآ اَيْدِيْهِمْ وَتَشْهَدُ اَرْجُلُهُمْ بِمَا كَانُوْا يَكْسِبُوْنَ

Today We shall seal their mouths and it will be their hands that shall speak to Us and their feet that shall testify as to what they earned.

COMMENTARY

If you have not practised to be connected with higher consciousness in this life, then after death you may not be able to. Life on this earth is a preparation for the next phase which has an entirely different cosmology.

Sacred Alchemy

84:7-8

فَأَمَّا مَنْ أُوتِيَ كِتَٰبَهُۥ بِيَمِينِهِۦ

فَسَوْفَ يُحَاسَبُ حِسَابًا يَسِيرًا

Then as to him who is given his book in his right hand, he shall be reckoned with by an easy reckoning.

COMMENTARY

If you live this life with constant self-awareness and self-correctedness then your real biography or the book that is being written for you, in you, upon you, within your own cells even, will be a book of ease, success and a welcome transformation.

Qur'anic Verses

23:103

They whose scales are light — these have lost their souls, and in hell shall abide forever.

COMMENTARY

The more you are concerned about your lower self, the more selfish you are. The more you are occupied with simple comfort and ease and survival, the less you are likely to be awakening to the inner garden and the more likely that you will be heading towards that which we consider to be hell.

Sacred Alchemy

19:40

It is We who will inherit the earth, and all beings thereon: to Us will they all be returned.

COMMENTARY

It is To Allah belongs the known and the unknown, heavens and earth. Therefore human beings, here for a short while, are like those who have rented a place or the body as well as the soul for a short while and all of it will return back to its original controller and governor. Do you refer to that whenever you are coming up with a new action or is it simply because you want it or you do not want it?

Qur'anic Verses

9:105

وَقُلِ اعْمَلُوا فَسَيَرَى اللهُ عَمَلَكُمْ وَرَسُولُهُ وَالْمُؤْمِنُونَ وَسَتُرَدُّونَ اِلٰى عٰلِمِ الْغَيْبِ وَالشَّهَادَةِ فَيُنَبِّئُكُمْ بِمَا كُنْتُمْ تَعْمَلُونَ

Strive, and Allah shall see your striving, as also His Messenger and the faithful. You shall be returned to the Knower of the invisible and the visible, and He will inform you of what you used to do.

COMMENTARY

Allah is the All-Knowing and our love of knowledge is for the love for Allah. Whatever you do, or don't do, is known and the more you are sensitive to He who knows it all, the less you will be committing errors that you will regret.

Sacred Alchemy

29:55

$$\text{يَوْمَ يَغْشَاهُمُ ٱلْعَذَابُ مِن فَوْقِهِمْ وَمِن تَحْتِ أَرْجُلِهِمْ وَيَقُولُ ذُوقُوا۟ مَا كُنتُمْ تَعْمَلُونَ}$$

A day shall come when the torment overshadows them from above them and from below their feet, and He shall say: "Taste that which you used to commit!"

COMMENTARY

And if you have not practised to go higher up in consciousness on this earth, the state of darkness that you are in will be your condition after death - that is an aspect of hell.

Qur'anic Verses

2:225

لَا يُؤَاخِذُكُمُ اللَّهُ بِاللَّغْوِ فِي أَيْمَانِكُمْ وَلَٰكِنْ يُؤَاخِذُكُمْ بِمَا كَسَبَتْ قُلُوبُكُمْ ۗ وَاللَّهُ غَفُورٌ حَلِيمٌ

Allah will not take you to task for oaths which you may have uttered without thought, but will take you to task for what your hearts have conceived: for Allah is Much-Forgiving, Forbearing.

COMMENTARY

As human beings we naturally fall occasionally in states of distraction, loss or errors. Also our intentions, what we communicate can sometimes be quite rubbish. What really matters most are the inner intentions of our own heart and that is what leaves its mark upon us; not so much the occasional mishaps.

Sacred Alchemy

3:25

فَكَيْفَ إِذَا جَمَعْنَٰهُمْ لِيَوْمٍ لَّا رَيْبَ فِيهِ وَوُفِّيَتْ كُلُّ نَفْسٍ مَّا كَسَبَتْ وَهُمْ لَا يُظْلَمُونَ

How will they fare when We gather them together for a day of which there is no doubt, when every soul will be paid in full for what it has done, and they will not be wronged?

COMMENTARY

At the point of death one enters a zone where there is no possibility to change or remedy anything. It is only in this realm that one can wipe out ones past.

Qur'anic Verses

23:74

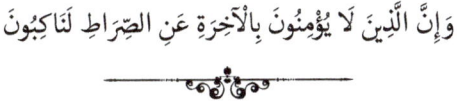

And surely they that believe not in the world to come are deviating from the path.

COMMENTARY

The ultimate guideline on this world is that life will come to an end and there is a direction which leaves us to full awakening and pure consciousness which is the state of the soul itself. The more you have faith and trust in this simple sketch, the more you are on the path of increase, joyfulness and reduced fears and sorrows.

Sacred Alchemy

Sacred Alchemy

www.ingramcontent.com/pod-product-compliance
Lightning Source LLC
Chambersburg PA
CBHW062022290426
44108CB00024B/2745